#FRUGALITYPAYS

Money Saving Tips For The Underachiever

*Written by
Antonio Starr*

Copyright ©2013 by Antonio Starr
All rights reserved.

No part of this book may be reproduced or utilized, in any form or by any means, electronic or mechanical, without prior permission in writing from the publisher except for the use of brief quotation in a book review where the author and book title are listed.

Produced by: Antonio Starr
A. Starr Enterprises
225 Main St #84 Hiram Georgia, 30141
Hello@antoniostarr.com
Antoniostarr.com

My Dedication Page

Completion! I love that word! As an underachiever for most of my life, it was very seldom that I would complete anything that took more than two days of dedication and focus. Not anymore. #FRUGALITYPAYS is now complete, and I have a few people that I would like to thank.

First of all to my lovely wife Erika who has always been my number one supporter in any endeavor that I ventured into. I know at times I sound really crazy with my ideas especially since I haven't completed a lot of them, but you never wavered as my support pillar. Thank you to my lovely kids Tatiana and Maceo who have to put up with my quirky money saving tactics that oftentimes make no sense at all to them. No worries, when you guys are married with kids something tells me that you will be quirkier than I ever was. To mom, dad and my sister I hope that I am making you guys proud. To all of my family, aunts, cousins, in-laws, I pray that when you guys speak about me it's mostly positive because I want to be a positive representations of all of our families.

I want to thank Amanda for helping me put this book together. You rock! To my good friend Lashelle... You changed my life when you showed me how to travel on a shoestring budget. I see this book as a way of taking some of what you showed me and paying it forward to the world. Lastly I want to thank my friend Rich for keeping me focused on this goal that we set together which is to be the next wave of thought leaders and inspirers to the world. We are on our way my friend! To all of my friends who have molded me into the man I am today, I sincerely thank you all. You guys have no idea how much I studied and emulated your drive and work ethic. I still do.

I'm a published AUTHOR guys! Even if I do not sell a single book, I completed this thing! I envisioned it, mapped it, worked it and finished it. If this 39 year old underachiever (at the time of publishing) can totally reinvent himself and do something that he never imagined possible, then ANYONE can do it! Thank God I lived long enough to change my way of thinking.

Disclaimer:

Neither the author nor any other person associated with this book may be held liable for any damages that may result from following the counsel in this book. No single book of financial advice can be used as a substitute for professional, personalized financial advice. Readers are encouraged to seek financial advice from qualified professionals, including accountants, attorneys and other qualified individuals. Some of the links in the book may be affiliates of the author. Although the author and publisher have made every effort to ensure that the information in this book was correct at press time, the author and publisher do not assume and hereby disclaim any liability to any party for any loss, damage, or disruption caused by errors or omissions, whether such errors or omissions result from negligence, accident, or any other cause.

Table Of Contents

Automate Bills and Other Payments……………………1

Automate Household Purchases……………………….11

Stop Buying Entertainment…………………………….17

Stop Drinking Bottled Water and Other Bottled Drinks……………………………………………………….27

Leave Your Credit Cards At Home……………………33

Be Conscious Of Where Your Food Money Goes..43

Make Clothes Buying Planned and Strategic………55

Optimize Credit Card Rewards……………………….65

Use Apps And The Internet For Easy Savings……..73

Be Flexible and Creative With Travel…………………81

Introduction

Many people think that saving money is hard to do, or that it requires hours of clipping coupons and dredging through sale bins. Part of this statement is true. Clipping coupons or what some call "Extreme Couponing" is a very time consuming process and, although it is very rewarding financially, some people just aren't able to dedicate the time needed.

A portion of these people have true scheduling conflicts while the rest of us are just a tad bit too lazy to take on this daily challenge. We are the Underachievers! In this book, I want to give my fellow Underachievers some of the simple money saving tips and tricks that I've learned over the past few years.

These tips may or may not save you thousands

of dollars (It's completely up to you), but we have to start somewhere, and one thing I know about us Underachievers is that we prefer quick and simple, or we will bail on the idea. Starting today, you need to make a commitment to yourself that you will take charge of your money. You have to make a personal resolution that even though you may fail to complete things on time, or even at all, you will follow these tips and embrace the frugality lifestyle. No more shall we allow our lack of research and follow through to cost us so much money. It is time to take charge of our finances! It is time to get Frugal because #FrugalityPays!

One thing that I despise are books that are full of fluff! I hate having to spend three hours reading a book only to realize that the author could have delivered the same message in a third of the time. With #FRUGALITYPAYS, I get straight to the point because my aim is to add immediate value to your life starting with the first paragraph of the first chapter.

Some of the tips in this book are more strategic actions as opposed to direct money saving tips such as buying from a clearance rack etc..., but if you can avoid late fees and other frivolous charges (i.e. finance charges), isn't that saving money too? Darn right it is! Before going any further, I must let you know that I am far from an expert at saving money, and light years away from being a financial "expert", but I do know that what is in this book works.

If someone had shared this information with me when I was younger, I probably would be an "expert" by now. My motivation to write this book is for people who have not been taught the power of money and how we must make an effort to stretch and squeeze every penny out of each dollar we spend. Some of you that read this book may not learn anything new from me, and that's because the book is not for you.

I challenge those of you who are more advanced at saving money to give this book to a person that you know can benefit from it. Especially those of you Underachievers with advance knowledge that do not want to invest time in teaching someone else these techniques (You know who you are).

I hope you enjoy #FRUGALITYPAYS and find some takeaways that can truly help you become that frugal money saving animal that you should be. Let's begin, shall we?

Chapter One

Automate Bills and Other Payments

AUTOMATED = AUTOMATIC

Almost every bank offers online bill pay, and most major utilities companies and credit cards companies have online payment options. It takes less than an hour to set up all of your accounts, and you will never have to worry about bills again. You also do not have to pay for checks and stamps anymore. You will not have to lift a finger once it is set up. How is that for a simple first step?

If you have your paycheck directly deposited to your checking account (which can help you avoid monthly fees), you can have the amount of your monthly bills transferred automatically into a separate account that is just for bills. This can also be a savings account, which earns interest on the money you have earmarked for bills.

For what it's worth *Our credit union offers greater returns on their checking accounts (with strict guidelines) then we got on a savings account at our old bank. Stop by your local credit union (most are open to the public now) to get more information before you commit to going the savings account route.*

Automating your paycheck can also help you build an emergency fund or save for a big purchase. When your paycheck is deposited, you can have money transferred automatically to a savings account. If you have just $50 deposited each paycheck, you will have $1,400 saved in just one year plus interest! (Assuming that you are paid bi-weekly) It seems like a small amount to cut from spending, but it will add up over time. When you do this, you are paying yourself first, and making sure that you are taken care of, whether that means saving for a new car, a house, or retirement. Pay yourself first, but make sure that you have something to show for it! That my motto (Thanks to my father).

SHIFT YOUR PARADIGM

For younger people, this may come naturally. Millennials are used to online banking, and many of them have never even had a checkbook, let alone know about how to record checks and reconcile your balance. For you, this advice will help you get started on a good financial foundation. You already know how to use the technology, and it is just a matter of putting it into practice.

For older generations, this advice may be a little more difficult. If you are accustomed to writing checks and feel a sense of security when you finish paying bills, it can be scary to lose that feeling of control over your finances. Do you remember a time when you forgot to sign a check or wrote it for the wrong amount? If you make this mistake with online bill pay, you can easily change it, and it saves a lot of hassle.

You can set alerts to notify you when bills have been paid so that you have that peace of mind. Your monthly "bill paying" time will be to the two minutes you check your email to confirm payment. This beats spending hours writing checks, addressing envelopes and recording the checks in your checkbook.

For what it's worth *Some companies offer a discount for automatic payment because they know you will never be late. Student loan lenders* *will often reduce your interest rate by setting up automatic payments. These concessions may not be advertised to the public, so don't be afraid to ask. The worst they can say is no.*

If you have credit card debt, you can setup recurring minimum payments to avoid any late fees or interest rate hikes (huge hikes!). Later, you can go back and pay more when you have money available. If you can afford it, set it to pay the entire statement balance each month, so you will not accrue any interest and you will prevent a debt snowball from accumulating on your credit cards.

Some banks will not charge you an overdraft fee on automatic payments, instead they will usually notify you and give you a 24 hour grace period to put money into cover the payments. Make sure to verify this with your bank. If your bank does not offer this service, set an alert a few days before the bills are so you can make sure that you have enough money and won't incur any overdraft fees. You can also set up overdraft protection, where the money can be taken out of your savings account or charged to your credit card if you have insufficient funds.

90% of our money problems are by spending money that we don't have. Have you ever looked up and thought "OMG I totally forgot about this bill and now I'm broke!"? If you know payments are coming, you may be tempted to spend a little less, so you don't have a money crisis in a few weeks. It's similar to writing checks. If you write a bunch of checks, you try and be careful, so they do not bounce.

The upside with automated bills is that if you do spend too much money, you can postpone a payment. Some companies will not charge you a late fee if you call in advance and request a one or two week grace period to pay your bill. You can easily check your balance, and upcoming payments online to see how much money you truly have.

I have all of my bills setup to be paid automatically every month. I can't remember the last time that I wrote a check or bought a book of stamps for bills. This is truly an Underachievers' dream come true to know that the work is being done for you in the background. Awesome!

Chapter Two
Automate Household Purchases

BUILD A SYSTEM FOR SAVING

You will always need toilet paper, dish soap, and other household goods. It is such a pain to have to remember to buy those items, and they can make your shopping trips very expensive. Even if you are buying the generic brand at the store, there are still other easier ways that can save you even more money and make it easier for you.

Instead of relying on yourself, your spouse, or a roommate to remember when you are out of important items, your computer can do that work for you. On Amazon, there is a feature where you can set those household items to ship to you automatically. This saves you money because Amazon gives you a discount - anywhere from 5% off to 20% off, and their prices are already comparable to stores like Wal-Mart or Target.

Who wouldn't want to get at least 5% off and not have to go to the store? Most of the products on Amazon are brand-name products, so you are getting more expensive and usually better quality products, but Amazon usually has the best prices around. If you have five or more items sent to your house each month, you can get an additional 5% off the cost of each of them. If you ordered toilet paper, paper towels, razor blades, hand soap, and your favorite cereal, you would be getting 10% off, and not having to buy them at the store.

It is very rare that you will find a store coupon for more than 10% off. Oh, and shipping is FREE on any "subscribe and save" product. If you find that you need the item more frequently or less frequently, it is easy to change how often you receive those items. This feature is one of the most rewarding I've ever taken advantage of on the internet as it has win wins everywhere.

I'm a fan of the set it and forget approach to life in general, so being able to subscribe to my necessities while saving money and gas at the same time is what I call a win-win.

BULK(LE) UP FOR SAVINGS

Another way you can save money on conventional household purchases is to buy in bulk. The best places to buy in bulk are warehouse stores like Sam's Club or Costco. You can either buy it all for one year, or do this every few months and split the purchases with friends or neighbors. They customarily have both name brands and generic brands, so you can choose which kind you prefer.

Make sure to compare unit costs instead of just total cost. These memberships cost money, but they can pay for themselves in a short time if you are smart about it. Not all of the products at warehouse clubs are a good deal. Some of the best things to buy include alcohol, paper goods (toilet paper, paper towels, etc.), office supplies, toothbrushes, and vitamins. Don't buy items that you won't use or items that will go bad before you use them.

The point of all of this is to make things both easier and inexpensive for you. You will get a better price if you buy online or in bulk. It is much more convenient to have these products already in your house, rather than having to remember to buy them all the time. They do not take up much storage space, and if there is some kind of emergency, you have backup supplies, as well.

Chapter Three
Stop Buying Entertainment

SUBSCRIBE, SUBSCRIBE, SUBSCRIBE

Entertainment is one of those discretionary budget categories where we tend to underestimate how much we spend. Brand new books, movies, and CD's (album downloads for the savvy) can add up pretty quickly. We all know that the public library can be a good place to get free entertainment, but they often lack new choices or have rented out what you really want. In this day and age it's all about subscribing for your entertainment you get endless options at buffet prices.

Check out music subscription services like Spotify or one of my favorites, Rhapsody. They are both less than $10 per month for access to a huge database of music. I am a fan of Rhapsody mainly because I can listen to or download full albums on demand including new released albums, LEGALLY. The beauty of these services is that you get unlimited music access for less than the price of one album from the store!

There are subscription services for video games like Gamefly where the price of one video game will get you nearly four months of unlimited access. Their library consists of practically every game available on every gaming system, and you can keep the games as long as you want with no late fee.

Netflix and Amazon Prime are excellent replacements for movies. Hulu Plus is a pennywise alternative for cable as many of your favorite TV shows are available on Hulu Plus the day after they air on television. With these types of subscription services, you are looking at $8 a month versus shelling out $125 - $200 a month to your favorite cable company. Do that math... Here I will do it for you:

$8 X 12 months = $96 a year for Hulu Plus

VS

$150 (median price) X 12 months = $1800 for cable service

That's an average savings of $1,700 a year! #FRUGALITYPAYS!

If you are like me, you only watch 10 channels max out of the 1000 or so channels that are offered so you will not miss much by firing these guys. If you think you absolutely can not live without cable, then call to cancel your service and see if they offer any deals. They do not want to lose you as a customer, and are usually willing to offer deep discounts if they think you are serious about bailing, so be prepare to present them with your very attractive offer from their competitor.

Call up their competition and tell them that you are thinking about switching, but only if you are getting an awesome deal. Once you haggle them down to a basement bargain price, go back to your cable company with this information. What you now have is leverage to negotiate your idea payment with the company.

If you can talk your way into locking this new rate in for at least one year, you will be good! Otherwise wash, rinse and repeat this firing process every 6 months or so to keep the price down, but I firmly believe that once you have a subscription service you will find that you use cable less and less frequently.

SHARE AND SHARE ALIKE

Back to libraries quick... The county next to us has what they call an E-Library, which is pretty awesome. In their E-Library, you can check out eBooks, eMagazines, Audio books, and other digital resources all from the comfort of your couch. This service is available free for residents of that county, but because we live in a different county, we had to pay an annual fee of $25.

This is nothing, compared to the money we will save in gas traveling to and from the library, not to mention the savings from NOT having to buy the eBook. I almost forgot to mention that their eBook selection is pulled from Amazon so you will have access to some of the newly released eBooks for free! This is potential savings of $100's of dollars a year depending on how much you like to read. Check with your local library to see if they offer a similar program.

You can also use the Internet to exchange your used media with other people. When you are done with something, you can pass it on to someone else and get something new for yourself. There are more than three million books on Paperback Swap, so there is no risk of not finding something. They also have an option where you can have books automatically ship to you a when it becomes available.

Earlier this year, I joined the site booklending.com to share eBooks with other like minded members looking to maximize our dollar..

On this site, you simply create a list of books that you would like to read, and when someone who owns that eBook makes it available to loan you will receive an email notification. The book will be yours for 14 days. No charge!

For those of you who still own CD's (like my mother) SwapaCD and SwapaDVD work in the same way. A great feature of this is that if you have credits on either of these sites, it can be transferred to any of the others. Therefore, if you do not want that CD anymore, you could trade it for a DVD or a book instead. You do have to pay for shipping (usually about $2), and you have to trade something first in order to get credits, but all of us have something trade worthy on our house.

If you really want to buy a certain book or movie, you could visit a used bookstore, but there are also websites that sell used versions. Thriftbooks.com is one good idea. They sell used paperbacks for under $5 each. Wherehouse.com is another website that lets you trade CDs, DVDs, and games. Amazon also sells used versions of some products. You can also use websites like Freecycle.com, where people give away items they no longer want. It does not require you to give away anything; they are just trying to keep trash out of landfills and reuse items.

For what it's worth *If you are a college student or someone that's financing a college student and you are paying full price for textbooks I feel sorry for you! Once my daughter gets her list of books needed for the next semester of college, the first place we hit up is the internet searching for either a great rental price or drastically reduced used textbooks. One of our favorite places for these deals is Alibris.com.*

* * *

In just this chapter alone, you can position yourself to put several thousand dollars back into your pocket if you so choose to do so. Again, being that I am a former underachiever I am naturally a fan of the set it and forget it approach to life, so subscription services make my life easier and my cost of living is lower than most people because of it. Can you feel your nest egg getting fatter and fatter? But wait, there's more!

CHAPTER FOUR

STOP DRINKING BOTTLED WATER AND OTHER BOTTLED DRINKS

WATER IS SUPPOSED TO BE FREE

BOTTLED water is expensive (ask my mom). If you buy a set of water bottles, you can keep them stashed in the fridge at home, and they will always be cold and ready to go. They are cheap enough that if you lose one, it is not the end of the world. My wife has been using the same water bottle for over a year now. You can also fill them with juice, which is also much cheaper bought in a big bottle than out of a vending machine.

You will not have to lug home big cases of water bottles, and they take just a few minutes to fill. Tap water is essentially free. Filling up your water bottles at home is not going to increase your water bill substantially. If you do not like the taste, you can always get an inexpensive filter.

The same applies to soda, coffee, and other bottled drinks. They really add up. If you have coffee in the morning, a soda with lunch, a sports drink at the gym, and then a mixed drink or a beer at night, you have spent more than $20 in one day just on drinks. Water is better for you for the majority of the time. You are looking at potentially spending $3,000-$5,000 a year just on drinks.

For what it's worth *Add that $3000 - $5000 savings with the $2000 - $3000 that you can save by subscribing to your entertainment, and you are close to $10,000 a year saved. AND! I haven't even talked about saving money on groceries and clothes yet.*

BE WEALTHY AND HEALTHY

OTHER drinks should be treats, not a regular thing. Many times, when we think we are hungry, we are really just thirsty, so drinking more water can also help you eat less food. Dehydration can sap your energy, and is hard on your heart, so drinking more water can help ease those problems. If you have to go to the doctor, this will end up costing you money when the prevention would have been free.

Water is also one of the best headache cures. If you are drinking too much coffee and soda, your stomach can develop digestive problems from so much acid. An easy and free way to fix this is to drink more water. The idea of eight glasses a day is not really scientifically founded, so just try to drink as much water as you can.

If you really need (want) those drinks, it can be cheaper to make them at home. It is easy to make a latte or cappuccino with a few cheap things. You can get a Moka pot for less than $10 to make espresso shots. You can froth milk and make foam in the microwave. The flavor syrups you get at Starbucks are just sugar, water, and artificial flavoring. You can easily make your own in the microwave at home.

The basic ratio is 2 parts sugar to 1 part water. If you want it flavored, you can use vanilla bean paste for vanilla, a cinnamon stick for cinnamon, or some pumpkin pie spice for that oh-so-famous drink that everyone rushes out to buy each fall.

You can make all of this in less time than it would take to walk or drive to Starbucks, and you will be paying only a fraction of the cost.

You can also make your own sports drinks, either by using the pre-made powder or by mixing sea salt, juice, and sugar. There are lots of recipes and ideas online for how to make your own drinks at home.

Chapter Five

LEAVE YOUR CREDIT CARDS AT HOME

CAN'T SPEND WHAT YOU DON'T HAVE

Most of us never think twice about carrying all of our credit cards in our wallet. Leaving them at home could not get any easier, and it will change the way you think about spending money. I remember receiving my first credit card when I was in the military. I had a credit limit of $300, and the same day that I activated the card, I went out and bought a pair of Timberland boots, which cost $120. Talk about a senseless purchase.

I would have never done that if I had been educated on the proper use of credit cards. Here's a good rule of thumb, if you don't have them, you can't use them. Leave them at home at least until you can discipline yourself enough not to use them frivolously. Carry around $20 for any small expenses you might incur while you're out.

There is very rarely anything over that amount that you NEED to buy right now. People managed to do this for hundreds of years before credit cards (or cell phones) were invented, so it should not be that hard to go about your usual day without a credit card.

There are some places that won't take a debit card or cash like hotels and car rental agencies, but not very many people have to spontaneously stay at a hotel. If you are going on a trip, it is always a good idea to have a credit card with you just in case.

Credit card debt is the number one reason

people spend too much money. Credit cards are very tempting to some people. It makes it too easy to impulse buy things that you don't really need or items you don't have. Keeping your cards at home will make you really think about a purchase before you make it.

It also helps you make your purchases intentional rather than impulsive. It is a good idea to wait 24 or 48 hours for a large purchase anyway. That will help you decide whether you really need something or if you were just caught in an impulse moment. I've heard about some people freezing their credit cards in a block of ice, so you have to wait until the ice melts (microwaving it will ruin the card).

I've never gone to that extreme, but whatever works for you, I'd say do it. It is okay to use a debit card or cash because there is more psychological pain associated with spending money now instead of thinking about paying for something later. Statistically, people who use credit cards spend more money than they would have if they used cash.

For what it's worth *Studies show that people who use credit cards have a harder time remembering how much something actually costs than people who spent cash.*

MIND TRICKS THE MONEY

If you are trying not to use a credit card, it can be helpful to write down all the things you want and can't buy in a little notebook or on your phone. Later when you look at the list and are not caught in the moment, you will realize how silly some of those purchases are.

Having a list of what tempts you can also help you recognize areas in which you might be weakest. Being frugal is not just about implementing these techniques of saving money, but being able to master the frugal mentality.

* * *

If you are really scared of being without your cards in an emergency, bring just one. Maybe one that you have had customized with an image that makes you stop and think before using it. Most companies will let you put your own image on the card for free. An image like this might do the trick:

This is a purposefully ugly design because spending all of your money carelessly is ugly! Another way you can do this is to put a blank business card on top in the same slot as your credit card. On that card, write something that you are saving for or write the total amount of debt you have on that card so you can remember why you need to spend less money in the first place.

For What It's Worth *I've made this image available for free to anyone that would like to use it for their credit card. Just go here* www.antoniostarr.com/ccimage*)*

Even if you leave your credit cards at home, it is usually better not to cancel them, especially if you have had the account for a long time. Those cards can boost your credit score, which can help you get a better interest rate on a loan or mortgage, and save you money in the long run.

* * *

Without getting into the art of effective credit card use to increase your credit score, I will just reiterate that credit cards do serve a beneficial purpose, but you must exercise a disciplined, frugal mentality at all times.

Chapter Six

Be Conscious of Where Your Food Money Goes

EATING OUT IS EATING UP YOUR BUDGET

EATING out at restaurants is one of the main areas where almost everyone spends too much money. I used to tell my friends "with the money my family used to spend eating out every month, I could have paid for a brand new Maserati". Eating out less is the best way to reduce food expenses, but it can be difficult if you do not like to cook. Cooking at home does not have to be difficult.

Stash frozen pizza or egg rolls in the freezer instead of calling for takeout (for the healthy eaters feel free to substitute the pizza and egg rolls with your favorite subsistence of choice). Bring your lunch to work instead of going out or you can do what I did once, which was to find a job that offers free lunch lol.

Even if you are getting help from the store (pre-chopped vegetables, jarred sauces, rotisserie chickens, etc.), it is still much cheaper than eating out every meal. It is okay to eat out sometimes, but you need to be aware of how much you are spending. Even replacing just a few meals a week can have a significant impact on your bank account.

If you have holes in your budget where your money is escaping from, I can almost guarantee that the biggest hole stems from eating out. It took me sitting down and doing some simple math to figure out just how much money was spewing out of my budgeting. To keep it simple let's take a look at a whole number example of how much money you are spending on eating out annually.

Working 8 hours a day five days a week I would eat out for at least two meals a day.

Breakfast on my drive in would cost roughly $6

Lunch typically ran me another $10

$6 + $10 = $16 a day on food during the work day

$16 X 5 days a week = $80 a week!

$80 X 49 weeks a year (allowing for vacation and sick time) = $3920 spent on food in one year! AND! This does not include dinner after work and eating out on the weekends. Let's look at those numbers now.

***

My family typically would spend about $200 a week eating out.

$200 X 52 weeks (even if we were sick we still found the strength to pick up food) = $10,400! A year! Remember that Maserati I talked about? Mind you these are modest numbers for what we used to spend.

$3920 + $10,400 = $14,320 Fourteen Thousand and Four Hundred Dollars we used to spend every year just eating out!

For what it's worth *Add that **$14,320** to the number mention earlier and that's nearly **$25,000** of potential savings in a single year.*

When you are spending money in smaller denominations you tend to lose track of the total damage until you look at your bank statement, but for most of us, there is an initial shock and then we're back to our old habits. When it came to eating out my underachiever mind would often take over, and I would convince myself "It is so much easier to pick something up than to slave in a kitchen for an hour. Plus I only know how to make Hamburger Helper anyway".

When you read that doesn't it sound like the silliest thing you've ever heard? That was really my mentality. Again my family, once you develop a strong frugal mentality you will not allow yourself to be how I once was. Below I will give you a few tips on how us underachievers can get motivated about cooking, so keep reading!

When you go grocery shopping, make a list. This helps you to keep focused and reduces impulse buys that can cost a lot of money. It will also help you to reduce food waste. Store or generic brands are usually cheaper than name brands and taste almost the same. Stock up, when things go on sale.

If you eat Cheerios every day and they are on sale for $1 off, and the original price was $3, buying it on sale will save you 33% of the food cost. If you can do that for all of your major staple ingredients, imagine seeing your total grocery bill at 33% off! Another benefit of stocking up is that if you are ever caught in an emergency, there will be some kind of food around the house to eat.

Also, when you are in the grocery store, be sure to check the clearance section, as you will often find huge savings on these shelves. Additionally, most of the food items are non-perishable, meaning they will not spoil, and I like that.

If you are a big meat and/or seafood eater, then

you should go to the grocery store first thing in the morning because this is when the meat department manager goes out and slashes prices on meat with a sell by date of that day. We typically save at least 50% on these items. I ask the manager to put another layer of wrapping on the meat; I take it home and freeze it for later consumption.

I'm not a doctor so you may want to consult with your physician before following this technique, but it works fine for us. This also works great for the fresh fruit bowls and veggie plates that most grocery stores sell.

For what it's worth Getting drastically reduced meats and fruits gets the official #FRUGALITYPAYS! shout out because I love these deals.

SLOW COOKING WITH FRIENDS

Invest in kitchen equipment that will save you money over time. The best piece of equipment for this goal is a slow cooker. Even the cheapest ones, which run about $30, still work well, and they last a long time. It is nearly impossible to break a slow cooker.

You can use them to make cheap pieces of meat into delicious and tender main dishes. It is great to just throw a few things in the slow cooker before work and have dinner ready when you come home. Another way a crockpot can save you money is that it uses less electricity than an oven so it will help reduce your power bill. Allrecipes.com has hundreds of slow cooker recipes that will make your life in the kitchen even easier. Thank me later.

Host an all day cook ahead party. Get together with a few friends and prep all of your meals for the month in one day. You can save money by shopping at a warehouse club or a restaurant supply store and buying items in bulk. If you don't have an appliance, like a food processor or blender, chances are that someone has the appliance and could bring it.

You will only have to wash dishes once instead of washing them every night. Make it a fun event. Have some wine and music playing and splurge on a fancy dinner afterwards to celebrate all of the time and money you are saving. You do need freezer space for meals, but if you store them in

Ziploc bags, you can fit a lot of meals in a regular freezer.

Chapter Seven

Make Clothes Buying Planned and Strategic

BUY WHAT YOU WANT BUT WEAR WHAT YOU BUY

The average American spends $1,700 a year on clothing. If that money was spent on the perfect wardrobe, it wouldn't be too bad, but most of us end up buying things that we never wear. There are clothes with new tags in almost everyone's closet. If you plan your wardrobe better and plan your purchases around that, you can save a lot of money.

The first big thing, only buy what you will wear. It is not a good idea to buy things that do not fit you right now. Do not go crazy with leopard print or other trends that you will be sick of in three months. Even if something is on sale, it does not mean that you need it. Avoid buying pieces of clothing that do not match the rest of your wardrobe.

Do buy things that are flattering on you, that will last, and that you like. We all have those pieces of clothing that we love and have had forever. If we treated all of our clothing like that, we would not constantly be saying that we had nothing to wear!

PLAN TO SAVE BIG!

The second major step is to plan your purchases for when you will get the most bang for your buck. Wait until the store is having a huge sale – they are frequently at the end of a season or near a major holiday. End of season shopping is when my family really racks up on clothes with huge savings. We can care less about whether something is going out of fashion according to the "experts.", If we like it and it fits into our wardrobe then we'll wear it.

```
temPrice 48.00        YouSave 37.36
PS SPORTSWEA 011335460247   G    11.88 T1
temPrice 49.50        YouSave 37.62
; COLLECTION 400918661469   G    11.52 T1
emPrice 48.00         YouSave 36.48
)RESS CLOTHE 400919154502   G    28.80 T
emPrice 160.00        YouSave 131.20
)RESS CLOTHE 790970285322   G    31.50 T
emPrice 175.00        YouSave 143.50

                      SUBTOTAL     324.42
   324.42 @  7.0%       TAX         22.71
                      TOTAL    $347.13


A DEBIT      XXXXXXXXXXXX2735    347.13
YMENT FROM PRIMARY ACCOUNT
PROVED            000000

         TOTAL SAVED: $1338.08


    THANK YOU FOR SHOPPING AT KOHL'S
```

This receipt is our actual receipt from the end of season shopping at Kohl's. We were able to get items at up to 80% off! This is just one receipt of the many that we have from catching end of season clearance sales (I saved even more than this at a Dillard's clearance sale one spring).

The key is to stay prepared for a great sale; which if you are implementing the tips already mentioned in this book you should be building a nice little nest egg of savings already. Being that you are purchasing clothing that is out of season (from a weather perspective not fashion because we can care less about that) you must have a vision of what you will need to add to your wardrobe when that season rolls around again. Remember even if you get something for 80% off if you are not going to wear it then you just wasted money.

Create a new email account and sign up for store emails, which will alert you to special sales or discounts. Store emails sometimes include coupons. Find more coupons online at stores like Coupon Closet, Coupon Sherpa, or Shooger. When you get to the store, you will be prepared to get a bargain. You can usually only use one coupon, but you can combine coupons with sales to get great deals on your clothes.

STRATEGIZE YOUR SPENDING

When you are at the store, there are things you can do to reduce how much you buy. Shop the perimeter and the back of the store first – the most expensive things are placed in the front middle. If your arms are already full when you get to the middle, you may be less tempted by those expensive things.

Use cash instead of credit cards. This will help keep you on a budget, and prevent you from overspending. It really makes you consider whether something is worth it if you have to count out all those dollars.

* * *

Online shopping can also be an easy way to spend too much money on clothes. However, it can also be helpful because you can avoid more impulse purchases if you go to a website knowing you are only there to buy a certain thing. You won't see all those other racks of clothes that you might want.

If you are more purposeful about what you need, you can avoid overspending. You can put alerts on different websites for when a certain thing goes on sale. If you add something to your cart, wait before you buy it to make sure you really want it. Amazon has a great feature called "save for later" that will create a list of all of the things you want to buy. Then if you do have money later, you can prioritize the things that are the most important to you and buy them.

CHAPTER EIGHT

OPTIMIZE CREDIT CARD REWARDS

KNOW PAIN. KNOW GAIN

Wʜɪʟᴇ credit cards can be dangerous and entice you to spend too much money, they can also be an easy way to earn money and rewards. The most important thing to remember about credit cards is that companies would not be offering these "great" deals if they did not make money off of them. They know that most people will not pay off their balances) each month.

If you find yourself carrying a balance, stop using the cards! The rewards are never worth the debt. Even if they give you a "free" $25 gift card, they are more than making up for it in interest and other fees they charge. As long as you are aware of this fact and proceed carefully, you can take advantage of those great deals and actually make money.

YOU MIGHT AS WELL GET PAID TO SPEND

Try to find a credit card that gives you rewards like cash back or points rather than gift cards or airline miles. Most of those cards do not give you any additional discounts on travel, merchandise, or gift cards, so you are having your money forced into something that you might not want to spend money on. A good guideline is to get three cents back per point. Anything below that means you are just wasting your money.

If you get cash, you can choose to buy those same things or you can use that money for something else. Sometimes you will get a gift card a little bit cheaper (you would have received $20 cash but got a $25 gift card) but remember, those are only a good deal if it is a place where you would have already spent money.

If you feel confident in your ability to exercise a disciplined frugal mentality, then there are ways to maximize your rewards every day without the pain of interest rates. I have a few credit cards that come with extra bonus points (double) on certain purchases like gas, groceries and drugstores so I use that to my advantage.

I buy all of the items in these categories on my credit card BUT I pay the balance off completely every month. As I said, you MUST have a highly disciplined frugal mentality to know that what you are charging on your card the cash to cover that cost is in the bank. Furthermore, you have to commit to taking this money from your bank account and paying the debt immediately otherwise you're stuck with a carryover balance and an interest charge that will pay the company back for the bonus points they gave you.

If you can master this art of credit card usage, then you will start racking up bonus points and/or cash without the risk of interest charges. Once you have accumulated enough points you can apply them towards free hotel stays, car rentals, flights, groceries you name it. Not to mention a huge improvement of your credit score because you will appear to the credit bureaus as a disciplined and responsible consumer.

For what it's worth *If your current credit card is not offering any type of reward program then I highly suggest you seek out another credit card ASAP, but DO NOT close your existing credit card* *account if you do find a replacement. It will hurt you more than it will help.*

Search for a debit card that gives you cash back. Many have special bonus periods where you can get up to 5% on groceries or gas. Credit card companies do the same thing and often have even better deals. Some companies will send you an email when they are offering bonus specials. For example, American Express will give you a $25 credit if you spent $25 on Small Business Saturday. That is free money - the only work you have to do is spend money!

You can have the cash back reward automatically applied to your balance to make your bill even lower, but check to make sure this is a good deal. It is not very flashy or exciting like a free airline ticket, but this is basically the credit card companies giving you free money and helping you pay your bills.

LET NO CREDIT CARD BENEFIT GO UNUSED

Credit cards can also give you other benefits like roadside assistance, extended warranties, or other travel protection. If your card has this perk, make sure to buy your electronics or travel bookings with your card so that you can take advantage of them. Some cards have a concierge service which will help you find discounts on travel and give you exclusive access events. Just make sure that you actually have the money and don't forget to pay that credit card off at the end of the month!

Chapter Nine

USE APPS AND THE INTERNET FOR EASY SAVINGS

APP(ETITE) FOR SAVING MONEY

There are lots of apps for your smartphone or tablet that can help you to save money. The great thing about all of these ways to find coupons is that you do not have to do very much work. If all of the deals are already waiting for you, you don't have to spend time looking for them.

Couponing used to take a lot of time. You had to get the paper, cut out the coupons and then remember to bring them to the store. It was hardly worth the time to do all of that work just to save a few dollars. But now, there are many websites and apps that will do all the work for you.

***

Instead of looking in the Sunday paper, you can use websites like Smartsource.com and Redplum.com. Coupons.com is another popular site, but you have to install software to use it. These websites let you pick the coupons you want and print them or use your mobile device.

Many store apps, like Michaels and Joann Fabrics, have weekly coupons right in the app, so you don't have to remember to bring the physical coupon with you. SavingStar, Grocery IQ, Ibotta, and Retailmenot are apps that give you coupons for lots of stores. Shopkick will give you reward points for shopping at certain stores, and you can redeem those points for gift cards and other items. The app Shop Savvy will compare prices with other stores and online stores so you can make sure you are really getting the best price.

***

I really like the apps that compare prices because they save me a lot of time and money by eliminating the need to drive from store to store searching for the best price on an item. As underachievers, we tend to not shop around because quite frankly it takes up to much of our time. Therefore, we are more prone to paying top dollar for an item that a little bit of research could have saved us quite a bit of money. Apps make the work smarter, not harder.

Don't forget about apps like Mint or Easy Envelope that can help you track spending! These apps can help you see where your money is going and keep you on budget. Having access to them right at your fingertips makes it easy to decide whether you really have the money for that latte or not.

If you use the Firefox browser, there are some extensions you can install that will help you save money. PriceDrop adds a button on Amazon that will automatically notify you if the price on something you really want goes down. RetailMeNot will pop up a bar that shows you if a website has discounts or specials, so you don't have to go searching for a coupon.

For what it's worth *If you get to the online checkout screen on a website and there is a field for a coupon or discount code, ALWAYS search for a code! A few minutes of research can often save you at least 10%.*

Gas prices are still through the roof so check out the gas buddy app. It uses your current GPS location to find the cheapest gas in your area. This really comes in handy when you are on a road trip or in a foreign city where you aren't aware of all the cheap (price) gas stations. You would be amazed at how much you can save per gallon by driving just another mile or two down the road. I once drove 8 miles off of the interstate to save 22 cents per gallon using gas buddy.

For what it's worth When traveling on the interstate the gas stations right off of the interstate are typically a lot higher than the gas station 2 or 3 miles down the road. This of course is unless you are stopping on a deserted exit with just one gas station (which I advise against for several reason).

EMAIL SUBSCRIPTIONS COME WITH COUPONS

Many big stores like Walgreens, Target, or even Whole Foods will send you a weekly newsletter with their ads and sales. That new email address that you created, set it up to filter these emails, so they are never in your inbox but go directly to a folder named "Coupons." Before you go shopping, you can just open this folder and browse all of the ads and sales in one place.

Many brands have weekly emails with coupons as well. If you sign up for their email ads, they will at times send exclusive coupons that you can't find anywhere else. You can create a separate folder for these brand-specific emails or just filter them into your coupons folder.

Many brands and companies have special coupons and promotions that are only available if you like them on Facebook or Twitter. If you are a regular user of these sites, it is easy to follow your favorites and see all the great deals they have.

For what it's worth *Another way to easily find coupons for a particular item is to Google the name of the item you want and the word coupon. If there is a coupon out there, it will usually be at the top of the list.*

Chapter Ten

Be Flexible and Creative with Travel

BE YOUR OWN TRAVEL AGENT

Don't depend on others to book your travel for you. Most of the best deals these days are online, and they are just as good as ones you can get from travel agents. You should figure out what part of your trip is the most important to you, and focus on making that happen. If staying in a really nice hotel is important to you, then don't spend money on expensive attractions.

If you really care about nice food, maybe you forsake buying souvenirs. The point is, be flexible about the things that are not as important to you. Travel guides wont always know what is important to you, and most of the plans you book with them are set in stone.

There are tons of good travel guides and review websites out there, which can help you easily find the best of what you want to do, and suggest cheaper alternatives to things that are less important to you.

If you keep your eyes open for deals, you can get a better price than a travel agent and have more flexibility about the things you do. Anticipating a trip is half of the fun, and planning it means you get to spend more time thinking about your trip.

FLEXIBILITY IS NEXT TO FRUGALNESS

If you are set on certain dates or a certain place, you will probably end up paying more money. Use things like the Explore tool on Kayak to search by cheapest destination. Try looking into substitute destinations like Quebec City instead of Paris, or Panama instead of Fiji. If you are willing to fly on a Thursday or a Monday, flights will drop by hundreds of dollars. Some attractions, especially museums, often have a free day, and planning your trip over that day can save you money on tickets.

When you are searching for the best deal, you don't want to have to search across 20 websites.

Sign up for special deal emails like Travelzoo.com or Airfarewatch.com dog to be alerted of the best deals and prices. Set up alerts for places you want to travel so you can get an email when the flight drops below a certain price.

CREATIVITY SAVES THE CASH

It would behoove you to search for vouchers before you travel. In 2012 I planned a father son trip for my son and I which consisted of traveling from Atlanta GA to Portland OR, Eugene OR (my son is a huge Oregon Ducks football fan), Seattle WA, Los Angeles CA, Miami FL and back home to Atlanta. Just taking a little time to search for a voucher I found out that Virgin America gave away free buy one get one free airline ticket vouchers at a San Francisco Giants home game earlier that year.

After a few minutes of further investigating I

found someone on Craigslist selling his vouchers for $25 each. Now I don't think that Virgin wanted their vouchers to be resold, but we live in a capitalist society, so I didn't mind. I was able to use these vouchers on our flight to LA from Seattle and from LA to Miami. My $50 investment saved me over $400! Always search for vouchers before buying travel, not to mention that you can buy drink vouchers for your favorite airlines among other travel perks.

Instead of a hotel, try staying at a hostel, an apartment, or with locals. Airbnb.com, VRBO.com and many other sites provide alternative lodging that is generally cheaper and more unique. While you're at your destination, check out deals on Groupon.com or Travelzoo.com for discounts on shows, events, and food.

If you are set on a hotel, try calling the hotel

directly for a discounted rate or use a price-bidding website to get a lower price. On the same trip I mentioned above, I used Priceline.com name your own price tool on all of our hotel stays, and saved an average of 55%. We landed a 5 star hotel in downtown LA for $99 a night through the name your price feature. I was stoked about that!

For what it's worth *If you take my advice on how to use your credit card rewards program to rack up points and cash then within a year or so you shouldn't have to worry about paying for a hotel room again. Just use your rewards. #FRUGALITYPAYS!*

Travel with groups. You can book a 10 person house for much less per person than you can book a 2 or 4 person house. This way, you'll get to spend time on your vacation with friends and family. You can get group discounts on transportation and tickets. It also allows people to do more of the things they want. Some people can go to the zoo while the other half goes to the party district.

Avoid souvenirs. They take up space, which means your limited luggage real estate. Most of the time, the stuff we buy is just stuff, and we don't have a place or a real use for it. If you want to buy something to remind you of a place, buy something that you will actually use.

If you don't drink tea now, don't buy a tea kettle thinking you will be that person who drinks tea from a fancy teapot. But if you do drink tea, that teapot might be the perfect thing for you. Other good souvenirs include artwork that you really have a spot on the wall for or food, because everyone eats, and most places have something that is particularly delicious and cheap.

Plan your vacation around inexpensive things. There are tons of free events and sights to see in almost every city. You will only remember parts of your trip anyway, so plan a few exciting and more expensive things at the end of your vacation. It gives you something to look forward to during your trip, rather than blowing all the excitement on the first day. Especially if you are traveling a long distance, you need time to recover and you won't enjoy a full-packed day right away. Use the first few days to get oriented to where you are staying, and spend time doing the cheap and local, low-key things.

With the way you've successfully turned your financial situation around and disciplined your frugal mentality after reading this book, you deserve a nice relaxing vacation. Enjoy.

IN CONCLUSION

When you take control of your money, you are gaining empowerment. You decide where you money goes, and you will have peace of mind if you are saving money. Even if you are the laziest person in the world, there is still a finance system that works for you. You can gain control of your finances and save money. These are just a few ideas that with a little bit of work can help you gain financial security. Most of these ideas require just some time up front, and they will put you on the path to better finances. So what are you waiting for? Get started on the path to becoming an Achiever of personal finance right now!

About The Author

Self-published author, Antonio Starr, enjoys sharing information to help people live life abundantly. Growing up on different continents and multiple cities around the USA has afforded Antonio the privilege of a multitude of life experiences to which he openly shares with his readers.

He writes Self-Help reference manuals as well as Fiction novels. For more information about Antonio's books, visit his website

www.antoniostarr.com

Be sure to join our community to receive regular emails of motivation, inspiration and informative content.

Find Antonio on **Facebook.com/speakerantoniostarr**

www.ingramcontent.com/pod-product-compliance
Lightning Source LLC
Chambersburg PA
CBHW051812170526
45167CB00005B/1977